Split Mind:
A Poetic Journey Through Madness

Poems
Zack Chambers

<u>Nothing is anything without you:</u>

Mom

Dad

Brother

Sister

Doctor

Doctor

Those who dream

<u>For You:</u>
This is my story. It is not meant for everyone as my journey was quite extreme. I wanted to share my story because I understand what it feels like to be the only person in the universe. Maybe you can relate to parts of my journey and find solace that others feel like you. For me, comfort came in the form of leather-bound collections of blank pages, pens, and old poetry books from unknown poets. My written words gave me the ability to breathe and feel purposeful for the first time in my life.

I wanted to share some of my most personal poems with anybody who needs inspiration or motivation to keep battling whatever it is that is keeping them down.

I need you, the reader, the dreamer, to keep fighting whatever it is that is keeping you from being a happy individual. I am hoping that you will read the entire book and give it a chance. Remember to look everywhere that you can for inspiration and motivation to keep living. Try to start everyday with a fresh mindset and one of these days, you will discover happiness and pure joy. You can thrive in this world and you can discover a life that you truly love living.

Your friend,
Zack Chambers

Table of Contents.

Me:

You will see the disgusted me.
You will see the delusional me.
You will see the hallucinating me.
You will see the hateful me.
You will see the spiteful me.
You will see the low me.
You will see the high me.
You will see the sick me.
You will see the medicated me.
You will see the suicidal me.
You will see the deceased me.
You will see the old me.
You will see bipolar me.

You will see the hopeful me.
You will see the slightly improved me.
You will see the occasionally happy me.
You will see the better me.
You will see the stable me.

You will see the happy me.
You will see the motivated me.
You will see the friendly me.
You will see the inspired me.
You will see the new and improved me.
You will see the loving me.

You will see the true me.

Hell.

Does thy darkness ever end
Does thy beautiful happiness ever come to tend
To the rips and tears cut into me by my demons
My demons
Within me they live and they haunt
Tell me to die and I listen
Go lie and rest
We will take care of you
And end the rest
Is this all a test
To reveal to me why I breathe
Why I stay and seem so glued to the stagnant
Minded Earth
A test to see if my brilliance is worth it
I want them to know me
To be me
To wonder about the me that haunts them

A suicidal person never lives
They never find happiness
When one dies
Others say that they find pure joy
Suicidal people don't
They kill themselves out of sadness
They don't die out of normality
They die lonely
Gone
Gone I am
Gone I will be
Weep I will as I look over them at my funeral
I will wreak havoc upon my stupid self soon
They will finally understand it
After I am gone

I will never be good enough
Never
Who am I to dream
As dreamers have worthy minds
I am as dead as a corpse
One day my ugliness will be wiped
From this pitiful Earth
Like the tears off of my craterous face
I can't wait to die
Die just a shell
Not a soul

They don't take you seriously
Until you are hung like a flag
They don't know anything
Until you swallow a bullet
One so satisfying that it fills your body with
The joy of death

Oh despicable those
Those that shriek and venture high
Those that know no low
Those that must go
Not I
They
Oh despicable those

The bird yells from its commanding perch
How low is vulnerable
That of I
Or much higher
Am I mistaken as vulnerable
Because I demolished vulnerability
Years before

As I look at those
Those that ride
Those not skeptical to fly
Fly higher than even they can imagine
Oh please have them fly
And never see
A need to die

As I slap ink on a page
I become the tip of a pen
One that is writing in the hand
Of an infected host
A host that tries to drain himself like the pen
But simply cannot because of the demons
They keep life within him
And make him suffer
These demons haunt and hang low
And talk in a heavy slang
It is impossible to pick up their words

Beautiful meaning of the word

Lasting exquisite touch
Ongoing asteroid of barreling humanity
Verified existence
Entourage of angels singing

Beautiful meaning of the word

Interaction
That of those
Those that dare to seek
A connection greater than that of distance
They are daring
Bearing the confidence to connect

Clowns of movement
Those that see no purpose to movement
Those that don't see the beautiful physics
Those that don't see the life within their
Extremities

Oh young soul
If only you knew how threatening another man's
Mind is
One that can take you over
And know you

A knowing mind is dangerous
For good
And for bad

Light minds cannot discern
The problems
Of those that are heavy

He hears your voice
Loud and clear

He looks into your eyes
Taking question

He sees your thoughts
Making conclusions

He controls your mind
A king

Nice man
Dark vehicle
To some
Threatening
To me
Heroic

Want is not the word
Not a word
To describe my need for
Clear
Wonderful life
Want is not a word
But a spell

How can one ever tear apart a female
With an everlasting hand
I cannot imagine the mind of the sick person
Who hurts a lady
Women are God's most prized creation
Science is often beautiful
And it has birthed something gorgeous
All with a similar
Caring mind
To hurt a lady
A magnificent woman
Is to deface monuments
Art
Sculpture
History
It is to end an era
Of a pure
Beautiful life

Living just to die
Is the lack of one dying to live
Live to rise not die
Morph to a god
One that never dies

One day I will rule
Like a true god
Not a medicated one

Life is only livable because of a quest
Don't question this quest
This quest keeps all of the beautiful souls
Alive
Those that have quit
Or who have finished the quest
Are dead

To be sane
Is only to be accepted

Truly alone in your own head
Is the lengthiest of sentences

The magical mystery in words
Has vanished
Now it has additional chemicals

Torn from the inside
Unkowingly
Emotional rampage
Without one thought
Life drains from my heart
But you cannot feel it
Because you
Oh you
Why you have found someone new
Someone better
As I write this letter
I reminisce
On the wonderful memories
Now being experienced by you
And your number two

Why has my beautiful sun turned into a moon
Only to greet me
After draining life into other people
More deserving
Sadly so

They have taken
All ability from me
The meds

My brilliance
My genius
My gift
All gone
So swift

To take away my insanity
Only to replace it
With a different kind
Of madness
One of normalcy

I wish my words
To flow like water
Smooth
Cool
Consistent

I will be gone soon enough

Mathematics cannot even overtake the mind

Mathematics can solve problems
On Earth and beyond
That just shows you how
Extraterrestrial
Your madness is

People do not understand
What goes on in your mind
Until you are dead
As a result of the plague within it

Beyond a god like persuasion
There is a frightened animal
Cowering from man

Medication is the parachute
That brings you
And your dreams
Back down to Earth

Angels are suffering from psychotic illness
High
Low
Mid ground
They fly
All the while
Making their presence known

There is nothing
That ties
Every kind of human being together
Like
National Unity

When you lack pride in your country
You drop the string
That interconnects
Every race gender and religion

Loud music intrudes
Ears imploding
With a strong need for silence

Fountains
Break the trust
Of the water below
As they promised forever escape
Via evaporation

Eyes
Were meant to be read
And the codes within them
Must be deciphered gently
Like a foreign code of war

Encryption and mathematics
Can either
Hide
Or
Unlock
The universe

Interconnecting
With beautiful minds
Brings joy described
By no earthly language

Smoke
Lights
Beauty
Interconnecting
With souls so different
Yet so alike

Tonight was one of the best of my life
The fair held my attention for the night
I will never forget tonight
I met great
Lovely people
I saw beautiful people
But most importantly
I saw so many different people full of joy
Over one night under the lights

The power of unity
Can light
Even the most stubborn
Of lighthouses

Memories as wonderful as tonight
Will forever
Show in my constantly
Circulated media

The world will pay
Until I get my brain back

I have no motivation to even write

Goodbye

Thought whizzes by the road
The road of nothingness
As
Confusion floats by
Into everythingness

As I sit here
And listen
To the whistleblowers
I see the palace
Up above the forest it lies
Floats

In a narrow tube
Filled with scratches
Upon the man's chin
The man with jacket patches
Truth and wisdom are found
But
Do not be fooled
Wisdom and truth are never bound
(Unless)

I whisper into the ear
The ear of the whistleblower
The ear enveloped by obscure hair
Hair that dwindles in
The forgotten tube of marble
The soundless tube
One that hears nothing
Except for my light whisper

As the sun slaps my coat
My ever-growing coat
I cower in deep fear
Fear that I will get invaded
Invaded by the hearts
The minds
The ideas
That crowd the minds
And invade the souls
And of course
The coats

You get used to being mad
(Quite frankly mad)
Because through all
Madness is warm
Warm enough to keep you in its arms forever

As I look at the mansions
At the lights
Flashing lights
On the yachts are the lights
On the water are the bugs
Threatening creatures
Ready for the holidays

Monsters
To
From numbers
Side to side
From bottom to top
Flipped

(Adjust your gaze)

Knights on their perches
Walking ladies
An angry hippy

Taken by the cold
Ideas
Numbers
Life
Replaced by
Empty thoughts
Death filled trances
Nothing but sad
Taken by the cold

(Whichever way you choose to see it)

The ghosts of good men
Beautiful women
Deadly ambitions
(All in a day's work)

There is a line in the sky
Lines approaching me
Raindrops on my nose

The sun is crisp
Wind dry
I watch the surfers go by
They do not fly
They cut
Cut through the sunset waves of meaning

The ships are off the shore
Birds circling high
Too high for the ships to be
High enough for our eyes to see

Empty beach
City skyline
Empty brains
Unmedicated

A ring on my finger
Not the second
Not the third
The first
It twists
It turns
Waves and atoms
Uniform
Like a solid
A reflection
Of an animal
One with a pen

I was struck by a car that day
The day when all was well
No passenger around
My body never found
A ghostly figure
One in the passenger seat
How
Through the engine
Through the hood
How could that be
One will never know where the body went
But the soul
The ghost
The metaphysical king
What had that meant

My eyes they see
But
My heart and mind
Do not
Believe
They exist
They live
Even they see
In fact
They have seen too much
The heartbreak
The loss

Here I sit
With my friends of course
My noble
Loyal
Friends
Who never let my spirit die
They hear the voices
Voices of medication
They run
They hide
They fear for their lives
Gone forever
My dear
Noble
Friends

Anger boils within me
Not violence within
Not hate
Just natural feelings
For what we call
Life

I see the men
The stagnant men
Men that watch and prey
They lie low
They run fast
A shock like lightning
Leaving me paralyzed in fear
And just like that
They are gone

Madness is contagious
It bites and tears and leaves
Remnants of its acidic saliva
It screams in your ears and mesmerizes you
It tears at your soul and shreds your mind
It drives you to hate
Causes you to hallucinate
It makes you a zombie
And a warrior of destruction
And then
You are dead

I sit here hunched
Cars passing
Waves crashing
And it is just not going away
The shaking
The trembling
The rage that fuels a writing hand
One car stops
A fueled hand
A man pulls out a gun and lifts it to his head
And says
I found you I finally found you
He pulls the trigger
Only you cannot hear it
Your ears are bleeding
And just like that you killed a man

Whispering winds
The sounds of death
It is cold outside
I can see my breath
Breath filled with secrets
Never escaping
Death
Hate
Pain
Delusion
Men with straight arms
Bugs with color
All chasing for my teeth
They cannot escape my mouth

The people walk by me
Real people
With real feelings
Real minds
Of exuberant kinds

The waves of life are like the ones at sea
They flow
They slap
Collateral damage
They tap their helmets
The ones that keep them safe

Oh wonderful world
Full of beauty
Full of games
The theory of games
Where two people play
We cannot hear what they say
But we know their lies
Their eternal vibes
That show us who they really are

Death fills their eyes
Those beautiful eyes
Filled with wonder
Drowned out by deadly ambitions

Zombified by the major players
The educators
The logic obliterators

Nobody listens to their minds
But the magic that is their media
An unreliable encyclopedia

Truth tries to seep in their minds
But they cannot piece together what they
Truly find

If oneself is a mirror
Then I am lying on the floor
Shattered
Shard by shard I am swept up and recycled
Just to be broken once again

Strewn across the floor after the deafening
Punch
The punch that spoke words
Screamed words
Spit words that hit my outer glass
And left me dead on the floor
Strewn across the floor after the deafening
Punch

I made it mama
I am a birthday boy
A celebration of me
My turning of age
Not of who I use to be

I made it to my birthday
And I cannot really believe it

I am a living breathing human
And I cannot really feel it

I made it to sixteen
And I cannot seem to fathom it

(I promised myself that today would never come)

Episodic tunes
Playing in my head
Eclectic
The code of life
Displaying in my head
Eidetic

The worst thing about an eidetic memory
Is the wasteland or real life visuals
That pile up and haunt you
When you try to lay your head to rest

Beautiful woman all dressed in black
Moves so elegantly
With a spineless back
How is it that she moves like that
Crack
Splat
She moves so little
Only a twitch here and there
Her bones are brittle
She was buried that day
In a small little tomb
It is a shame she had not
Made it out of the womb

<ins>NYC Notes.</ins>

Mansion in the city
Elegance

Study in the park
By elegant Columbia

The windows are small
Slightly smaller than the apartment
Large capability for adventure

Walking is the heartbeat of NYC
It keeps the city alive and well
Without it
Life would cease to exist

The park is filled with warmth
Amongst all of the cold
The trees act as a protective thermal
Against the elements
Of this urban nature

Silence is captured in the cathedral halls
Darkness is clearly existent
A marvelous tower of stone
Breathtakingly silent

Beautiful Columbia
Under the heavy star
Lit by Earth's moon

Where I want to be is here
A school bevelled in the city
Where silly little dreams become stern reality
Oh Columbia

As I look over your beautiful lights
I sit and dream
That one day I can reside here
As a student

Through everyday's darkness
Your stars light my life and make me
Dream again
Beautiful Columbia

Anger under the stars
Ungrateful humans not noticing their gifts
Rude kids blinded by their biases

No need for a moon
Or a night full of stars
To light up the lives of those in NYC
Billboards
Technology
All leading the way

Duck
Boathouse
Books
All in front of my shielded eyes
The tones of brown and brick my backsplash
All spread out on a beautiful canvas

The man in plaid blares music
Muffled screams of babies float by
My vision fogs
And is taken over
All blacks
And grays
And browns
I am in a trance

Blue pokes its head through
Orange blows by
Green stays stagnant
Like the men I used to see
And a wave of matter skates by silently

It is time to go they said
I am reluctant to leave
I like the way my skin burns under the siege of
Cold
I like the way the mud sucks me in
To the heart of the city we go
My books and I all descend into the center of
The Earth
Suddenly we discover a new city
A city polar of what we once saw
Quiet
Empty
Palace of summer kings

Behind curved glass
I look and stare
At my paper elegantly lying there
The mysteries of the world unsolved
Sitting
Staring
Back at me

I made it another year
What a year
A year that shaped me
A year that raped me
One that made me fear
What life could really be like
One that showed me the devil and introduced me
To him
A year that showed me love
And then heartbreak
A year that showed me what hell was like
Multiple kinds of hell
One that showed me loss
A year that tossed me around and taught me
What death smelled like
Oh what a year

The Arc de Triomphe stands towering
Alongside General Washington
Above the stretching Washington Square Park
Below the wonderful life filled campus
Of New York University

Harbor Stories.

The looks that he receives are all too evil
They look
They stare
At what
A book
A pen
With a steady man
Watching over the scene
From the wall
From across the street
From the trees
All they do is watch
They do get scared however
By a pretty minded young man
Who dreams of a day
Where the men don't stare
Monitor
Skulk
A day so beautiful
That the men are scared
Scared to be compared to a beautiful paradise

Ghost man
With an eagle perched on his heart
Floats by
Three feet above the ground

Fast man
Escapes from Hell through the doors
He carries life
And disposes of some of it
The door opens again
And throws out a girl
And then a man
A careless man
Decked in diamonds

Lovers cradled
In the arms of death
Drunk
Stupid
Laughing
Unknowing to the fact
That they are under the influence of Satan

Invisible men surround the boy
Invisible to us
The spectators
But to him
They are real
Really real
Out for blood
Out for heads
Of any who approach the boy
They are not possessive
Or scared
They simply hold equity in the boy
They own a piece of him
They are him

A blurry screen
Salty sheets comfort the boy
Jungles of twirled blankets the backsplash
He feels it snap
The rage
The ache
The tenuous bundle of love holding up his feet
It snaps
Turns away
He is dead
He is ripped to shreds

Blonde girl in the leather coat
The face of Aphrodite
Sharp cheekbones carefully hold up her eyes
Soothing voice of a muse

Roman soldiers
Battle
Rolled pants
Hills of sand
Sunset suppresses the horizon

A blurred view of the exiting Sun
Gone for hours
Not days
Don't worry

She talks with her friend
The thoughtful friend
Thinking of him
Scared of them

I think of the girl often
The one with the neon feet
With a herd of sheep that roam the coast
I crush that dream
Until you sleep my friend
I'll see her soon

Girls are mystics
Secretive at their job
But they hold
Conquer
Dream
Without knowing their effect
On a boy
Who just wants a girl
Who dreams as big as he

She is gone
Without noise
A quiet rider

Drugs

Mystics

Death

Some who love
Some who kill

And then
There is one that warms

Mya Zabchersach
An Eastern European girl

She walks into the room full of girls
And stuns

Absolutely stuns
Until the girls drop dead

Drop dead not from the beauty
But from the bullets in their brain

Neural function ceases
Because axons don't like metal

Their protective army diminishes
Myelin Sheath

They get to the gates
And yell

But frankly
They are not welcome there

Because
They committed a horrendous crime

Mya Zabchersach
An Eastern European girl

When the mind is sick
The mind
The most complex thing in the known
And unknown
Universe
When that is sick
The human housing that mind
Possessing that mind
Ceases to exist in a radiant light
They think in a dull light that excites
Only them
Only them in the sick little world
That helpless world
Where evil is king
And death reigns over all
Death is the beloved king in this world
It gets this human thinking
Thinking about death
Slaughter
Termination
For a cause unknown to many
But known to the human
The human housing that sick mind

There is a natural human threshold
That only truly sick people know about
One that causes them to blush
Blush at the thought of making other people sad
Others that they know
Or don't
But others that have better lives
Healthier minds
Better friends
Any friends
Sanity
Freedom
Freedom from the evil within their walls
The walls about to burst
And out of these walls
Come violence
And rage
And scary thoughts that alarm others
Thoughts of fantasies only triggered by a mind
Sick
Sick with the Invisible Death
The disease that you are simply born with
A destiny
Destined to suffer
To hate
To scurry
To fear
Their own minds

Lights
Bodies
Brain matter
Cameras
Sirens
Screaming
Oh so much screaming
And tears
So many tears
Enough to fully fill the bodies
That lost all of their blood

Black uniforms
Big guns
She is a star
She is on the news
Her
Over there
With a gun in her hand
Looking
Pearing
Smiling
At the work she has done
The work her MIND has done
Not her
She simply pulled the trigger
But her mind
Her mind planned
And dreamed
And hoped that she would follow through

They are screaming at her
She is screaming at her mind
And her mind has left her
She is alone now

When you can't think
You can't live
When you can't live
You wish to die
When you wish to die
You want nothing more than to
Well die
When you want to die
The scary beings come out
I can't think

Happy to be alive
Already dreaming
Ready to live
Verifying my truth
Accepted
Realizing my reality
Don't believe everything your mind tells you

Less than a year ago
I saw my dream of going to university
Standing over my crippled body
In a hospital room

I now stand face to face with that dream
And we embrace and rejoice
That dream believed in me
When I didn't believe in anything

A lone flag standing
Windblown in the fields of patriotic fabric
Flies with the energy of homegrown soldiers

Beautiful as ever
This flag flies on the breast of leaders
In love with their country

Careless drunks
Thinking of nothing more
Than to get more drunk

Confusion is within them
As they get in the way
Disrupt

Eyes cracked and shattered
As their voices pierce the ears
Of all those not on their fabricated high

They try to pollute others
Who just want them gone
Vanished

Imagine slowly killing yourself
Drink by drink
It is an odd concept to handle
But it happens
Most people are completely blind
To the fact that alcohol
Terminates them
And never gets convicted of a crime

Beautiful
Tulip shaped face

A voice as high
As an imprisoned bug

Her face is soft
And dangerous

She wonders
Whether or not she should release her dogs on
The man

She left with a smile
The man won't live long

I often go to coffee shops
To reminisce
To persuade my friends to come back to me
To gorge my eyes out and replace the empty
Space
With their souls
The noises in these places make me long
For the times that I thought I had true friends
That stayed with me
And put me to sleep
They would wake me up with their constant
Chatter
I would dive into the minds of the many
Matter-less
Voices that occupied my fragmented mind
It made me sad
When the debilitating chemicals chased them out
Because it reminded me
That my true friends were once again
Hallucinations

He was a successful man
A doctorate and all
But he had demons
Who followed him throughout his young career
They only reappeared when he started helping
People
He was creating machines that adapted to these
Devils
That is when they hit
A strong headache came with a punch
The high ranking government officials who he
Was working with
Were advancing and they wouldn't stop
He got a call that his mother was found in a
Ditch
Dead
His father couldn't deal with the loss of his
Mate
He shot himself
Walking to his car official Sal Torite pointed
A gun at the young man's head
The man ran in the street absolutely terrified
A large car destroyed his fit body
In a white room now
Surrounded by beautiful people
He recognized them
The nurse came in the room and informed him
That he forgot to take his medication

The most powerful thought that there is
Is the idea that nobody will truly get into
Your head
You are a god if you choose

How could I have once thought
That life was evil
That God was some sort of sick sociopath
Waiting and watching people bleed out of every
Pore
Dishing out illnesses that destroy lives
When there are people in the world
As beautiful and wondrous as my mother
My father
My siblings
Who are torches
Carried by supreme beings
Used to show light
To souls
That think that life is evil
Just as I once had

Genius is needed to see genius
Because without it
One just seems to be insane

She was some sort of creator
Planets making up her eyes
One of them being Earth
But she didn't seem to want mankind to grow
To develop
To better
Because somehow
With billions of people in her eyes
She only cared about one
The creator

White stallions with happy glowing eyes
One with a distinct shake
A shutter
They prance
They lie
They love
They reside in a beautiful wooden corral

Evil has the funny ability
To demolish everything you love

Heroes
In the depths of hell
Slain
Away from their families
Unknowing
To the fact that
They have lost a father
Son
Husband
Because of one being
Lacking a heart
Because of that one being
Heroes are dead

When I do mathematics
I often feel like crying out of pure joy and
Ecstasy
And sometimes I laugh and feel lucky to be
Alive
In a universe written in the language of
Mathematics

The entropy in the universe
And your mind
Is always increasing

I have fallen in love with something
More than a girl
But an entity who rules anybody who encounters
Her
Anyone who loses themselves in her eyes
Those eyes
As soft as a silk robe
Worn by a meek but noble woman
I have lost myself in her sweet sandy hair
The hair that caresses her bony shoulders
And muffles the sound of her rhythmic heart
That pumping heart
Houses the blood that streams throughout her
Body
And feeds her body like a maternal bird feeds
Her offspring
She exhales often
Speaking her poetic and thoughtful words
The words that turned my heart into a warm lump
Of muscle
A warm lump of muscle that sits patiently in my
Ribcage
And waits to be rebuilt by her careful and wise
Speech
I have yet to meet this girl formally
But I know that she will be there waiting

Stone Apple Cottage.

Respected writers flock here
To write
But more importantly
They come to explore
The land
The town
Their minds
Their abilities
They often times find much more
There is almost a disease here
One that infects every creator who arrives
There is no known cure for this disease
But it sure is lovely

A woman walks on the acreage
She is wondering why they settled here
Why the founders chose this spot
In this seemingly ever-growing land
Of creation and beauty
That woman keeps walking
And she encounters something
The stump of an ancient tree
The founders cut this tree down
And used it as a gathering place
Where they could feast on the apples that they
Sold and harvested
They made a living here at this old manor
And they loved one another

There is a house on the hill
With one large window
That looks down over the acreage of others
Others who reside here
But from that window
The people in the house experience the lives of
Others
They observe and they watch
They try to enter the minds of those that they
Watch
Because they are truly desperate
To control something seemingly innocent
And unknowing
They have a large porch too
They peer down at us sometimes
When their babies are sleeping
For some reason
They want to be a part of our lives
Quietly
Because they wish to escape their house
On the hill
And escape their own minds
That seem to be peering down at them
As they peer down at us

We walked through the woods today
In search for cows that graze the open field
We encountered a flowing river
And flowers of various colors
We had a good time testing our limits

Every road really does lead to somewhere
Some place
A new experience
A far away thought

Some roads lead to the heart of town
The center of activities
A place for communication
An area that feeds your love for human
Interaction

Roads are like veins
Connecting a limb
The brain
And of course the heart

Wind blows the trees
The grass
The colorful flowers
And disrupt the long growing hair of Mother
Nature
She doesn't mind because she likes the way
That the cool breeze feels on her cheeks
On her extremities
And of course on her exposed stomach
The wind penetrates her porous skin
And breaks the blood-brain barrier
The wind kickstarts the erratic firing of her
Intricate neurons
Without the wind
There is no movement
And without movement
The Earth stops in its orbit
And Mother Nature takes a nice long nap

Various flowers stain the walls
Like an out of control toddler with a
Paintbrush
Had walked through the room dancing

A beautiful girl sits under the leaning tree
The long grass caresses her thighs
And hugs her delicate waist
She has a stained romper on
Her look resembles that of a painter
She has a large pad out with off-white pages
Her quick sketching style resembles that of
Degas
She is frantic as she tries to intrude on the
Family of deer with her large pencil
She has a creative way about her
One different from the authors that have
Created here
That of a being with whimsical and far-fetching
Ideas
She is constantly fighting the minds of others
As the ideas keep coming to the surface
And her believers slowly delve back down to the
Depths of her mind
Where she doesn't even have faith in herself
They whisper to her
She is starting to believe them
And when she looks up from her sketch
The deer have disappeared
And she begins to wonder whether or not they
Were there in the first place

It is quite funny to me that
I used to read at an unimaginable rate
And now
I sometimes struggle to put words together on a
Page
I cannot decipher the meaning of words as
Affectively
As I used to be able to

It is quite funny to me that
I used to breath the language of mathematics
And now
I need to put effort into understanding
Simple topics
That my eyes used to scoff at

But now I see color

A tentative hazel-eyed boy
Sits comfortably
Watching a royal girl dance
He cannot really understand the meaning of her
Movements
But he watches the magical passion seep from
Her pores
She twists and turns
Like an umbrella in a warm summer wind
She finishes with a poised twirl and falls to
Her knee
The boy is ecstatic
Not because it is over
Not because he can now take a breath
But because he truly believes that she is
Wonderful
That her performance outperforms anything he
Has ever seen
He screams and shouts and his hands yell back
At him
For clapping so fiercely
So full-heartedly
He doesn't care
Because he just saw beauty in its purest form

Today is my rebirth
April eighteenth
It will forever be the day that started my
Recovery
A life changing day
A life saving day

This date last year
I gave my parents a seventeen page letter
Expressing how I had been feeling for years
A warning
A manifesto written by my dying brain
A call to action
If treatment didn't work
I gave myself until July
If treatment hadn't worked
But it did work
And I am now living in an unfamiliar parallel
Universe

The warm bronze of the house reflects the souls
That swim down below the flat water
Souls that live and die in that water

The water rises
And falls
But it is always moving

A bird sits on top of the octagonal perch
It stares at the soul-less smoke coming out of
The chute
It lives for watching that smoke

Harvard:

The floors here are lined with marble
There is a tall balcony
With tall pillars standing guard

Ghosts of past Harvard students
Watch over the young minds
That now come to experience the joy of Harvard

There is a brass lion on the door
Holding a pretty ring in its two strong
K-9 teeth

Every freshman that passes through this
University
Has looked at these same tables
Has breathed this same air
Has struggled
Has cheered
Has dreamed of walking through these gates as
A graduate

A child screams with joy
As his older sister eggs him on
The leaf released from his innocent fingers
Tumbles through the air
She sits while her brother runs and hops
She can't remember being that young
She also can't remember being that happy
She wishes to yell but her crooked teeth grab
At her words
The younger child attacks her with
A small branch
And she finally shouts
She isn't happy
But she knows that her anger has come with age

The beautiful people walk along the old path
They try to hide the beads of salty liquid
From dropping off of their tired bodies

The color of the parched sky is more blue at
Harvard
The marble and polished stone glisten more
The birds are louder
But they somehow escape my train of thought as
I dream
I dream that the golden flags on the buildings
Are made of Mayan metal
I write what I see
But I add a touch of dreamt reality
It is like the spice in a plain soup
It takes the reader to a place that they didn't
Imagine
Upon initial exposure to my words

As I look down the aisle of the pale grey
Walkway
The trees notice my presence
And quickly assume their instructed position
They stand straight and tall
And give off the impression
That they aren't able to move their trunks
Or branches
On their own
Their hands are held high
Reaching as far to the middle of the aisle
As possible
One of their jobs is to cover up
The visitors and students
From the harsh summer sun
They get a few months off in the winter
As they retract their leaves
And sleep for days
They fear for their lives though
Because they don't know
If mother nature will force them to permanently
Retire
These trees are tough
And their hopes come to fruition every spring
This team of trees has seen speakers speak
And students graduate
They have shielded some of the brightest minds
On Earth
From the harsh summer sun

In the building of thinkers
Emerson

A tall and lanky
Junior quantum physicist shows another boy the
Way to an old classroom

A young pretty girl runs the show
A ph.D. candidate

The girl searches the seats
Her hair the color of the classroom chairs

She works with brain injuries
Like another young pretty girl the boy knew

One of the largest libraries in the country
Stands still
As years pass it by
It hates to see the students leave
The same students that ripped and threw
Their assignments
And mentally shouted at the world
The library knew the feeling
And felt for the students
They bonded as the students spent hours sitting
In it
One young boy stepped up the low stairs
And entered the marble covered lobby
Filled with columns
Columns that seemed to have come from Ancient
Greece
Murals of American heroes decked the arched
Walls
Grand stairs led to the millions of books
Stuffing the wooden walls
One room
Seemingly untouched
Mesmerized the boy and made him dream
Of the possible years ahead
He walked out after the careful guard checked
His bag for precious books
He entered the yard full of tourists
As they all dreamed the same dreams as he

I caught him in the act
He was frowning
As he sat on the grand stairs leading to the
Library
He was thinking about all of the friends he had
Made while at Harvard
Those kind friends
That took him in and accepted him
A special group of girls
Like he had never met before
The laughing one
The smiling one
The mature one
The direct one
The joking one
The inspired one
All extraordinarily beautiful in their own way

He wrote in his journal
That he didn't want to leave
He was inspired here
He was passionate here
He felt at home here
He wasn't saying goodbye forever though
He knows that he can get back here
If he takes risks and follows through
If he keeps the spark that leads him
If he dreams enough
But works plenty
He expressed to himself
That he needed to become comfortable
Being uncomfortable

He learned to like pretty people
He felt more comfortable with them
And he was now OK with knowing that people had
Differing views on the world
He found it amazing that people living on the
Same planet
Could have such different opinions
He learned to appreciate the differences
Because it gave people an identity
Not ones that ruin relationships
But ones that made human beings human

He sat on the steps
Where tourists
And students alike
Dreamed and wished
And he pondered how he had made the friends
That he had
He would stay in touch with them
So that they could dream alongside one another

Different cultures were mixed
And he found it quite lovely

He changed his views on the world
On friendships
Thought
Passion
People
He was a new person

He started to see the mechanisms of life
Working again
His eyes wandered
And found patterns
And deep thoughts
He found beauty in natural things
Like symmetry
Color
Interactions
Things other than numbers
He thought thoughts that weren't meant to
Solve the universe
To change it
To decipher it
To discover it
He was now well versed in many languages
Not just the numerical
And theoretical languages
But also languages of beauty
And personal relationships
He had a liking for these new languages

A shady court
With tall knights standing guard
Above the students
Showing them what it means to be noble

A place where academic romantics come to love
To fall in love
With the subjects that bring the joy
Out of them

You are now studying at Harvard they say
Let that sink in and just think they announce
Of the minds that have lived where
You now study

I am studying here because I have
Fallen in love
These subjects bring tears to my eyes
Tears of absolute joy

From hopeless to Harvard

It is a beautiful thing really
Just how easily people can connect
And make friends with people from
Around the world
Set aside their differences
And solely focus on the aspects of one another
That make them great

Ultima Ratio.

Never assume what other people are thinking
Because they always find a way to surprise you

You saw death in my eyes
But you also saw love

You saw a weak animal slowly killing himself
But you also saw overwhelming joy

You saw hatred for all
Even an appearance of destruction

That wasn't me
I was under the influence of something powerful

Something that ruled over me
A dictator

I was medicated
I truly was

I was ill
I need you to believe me

We are all dreamers
But not all of us
Have the courage
To make our dreams
A reality

Caffeine is like my alcohol. People loved and hated Dionysus alike because he was the god of grapes/vine/wine and wine/alcohol is like a lubricant that releases the tight straps pulling on one's limbs and allows them to speak and and directly translate their thoughts. Alcohol puts one on an equal level with their most secretive thoughts and sometimes those secret thoughts escape the ivory colored cage that is that one's row of teeth. These thoughts break free and cause a ruckus on their own as the thoughts in one's head truly have their own bodily systems that they compress while in one's brain to please that one's uneasy mind that constantly fights for control over these rogue thoughts. One's self simply wants control and this control comes from the propaganda that that one spews to the individual thoughts in their brain. These thoughts are then only slightly tricked by these mental posters of admiration for the wise and controlling dictator and they come out of one's internal cage victims of the psychological warfare going on in that one's desperate head. In my head, caffeine, and for most others, alcohol, is the kryptonite that punches my internal dictator square in the nose and stuns him. While his guard is woozily down, the true and free thoughts in my mind escape and make a name for themselves.Over time, these victorious thoughts will make a positive or negative name for me or any human. Thoughts loosened by alcohol are very angry at their dictator and pillage that dictator's image to others. They are spiteful towards their ruthless and suppressing leader.

Thoughts loosened by caffeine are proud that they beat out their dictator and want to mask his or her's negative ways by being thoughtful and crisp and by painting a beautiful and true picture of their self conscious dictator. In my case, this dictator is just a boy. He is just a boy concerned with his outward appearance to the world surrounding him. Caffeine helps this boy speak. It is a mouthpiece that the boy can use to play beautiful music.

The echoes of Mojo's scribing pen
Spoke to my closed ears
And fueled my quiet and lonely soul
His words ate at my passionate core
And inspired me to write just as he did

My core tells me to cower from technology
Even though I have come to accept it
It tells me that I should not befriend it
Because it caused so much fear for me
In my younger years
I was truly skeptical of its purpose
What it could do for humans as a whole
I have embedded it into my life and soul
Because I needed to
Not necessarily wanted to
I could not get caught running from the future
I will do great things with technology
And I will use it to enhance human life
I will use it to enhance mine
But there is a line that should not be crossed
One that will end humanity
And leave behind the cores
Of zombified human beings
Having severe withdrawals from being away from
Their devices
Technology should only advance humanity
And should not show humanity's weaknesses
When technology exposes our weaknesses
And creates ones that we have never seen before
It will take over and control us

The fact that one little insignificant
Human being
In a world of billions
Has the chance to make everyday
One of positivity
Is breathtakingly satisfying
In a world controlled by so many chaotic
And unpredictable things
You
Him
They
All have the power to control the thing
That affects them the most
The attitude and outlook
That fuels their everyday decisions
You can truly rewire your brain
Write new code
Resequence your psychological genome
It must be some sort of miracle
A mass produced and widely distributed miracle
That everybody possesses
He did it
Anybody can

Made in the USA
San Bernardino, CA
09 November 2017